Eli Learns
to Act Like a
Grown Up
Be Smart with Your Art!

Written by: R. Gold

Illustrations: Nechama Liebler.

Translation and Rhymes by: Shoshana Lepon

Designed by: Rachel Yagel

goldbsd@gmail.com | goldbsd.co.il

Grandma brings a gift.
What can it be?
Eli can't wait
to open and see.

Lots of crayons
with colors so bright.
"Thanks!" says Eli
and hugs Grandma tight.

He takes out a crayon
and draws on the wall.
A red house, a yellow man…
It's not hard at all!

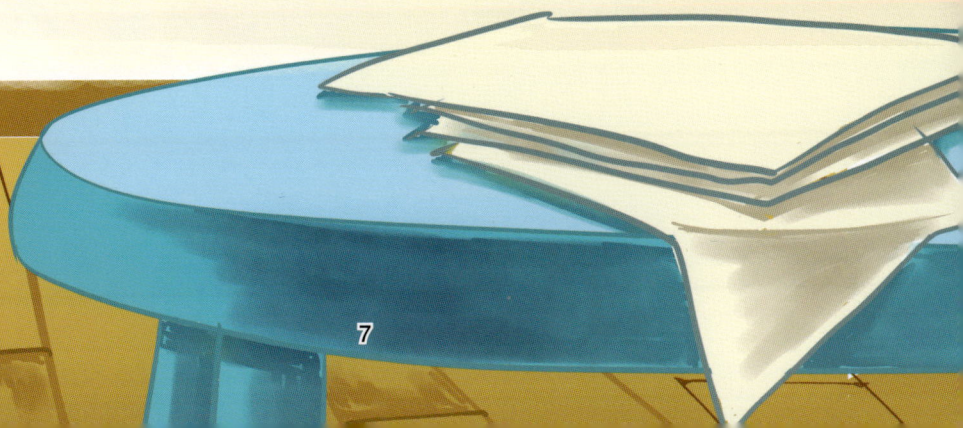

But Mommy comes
and she's not glad.
She says,
"Coloring on the wall is bad!"

Before Shabbat
the guests come in
and say to Eli
with a grin,

"Drawing on the wall? It looks
like you finished all
your coloring books!"

Mom gives Eli
soap and a cloth.
He scrubs and scrubs
but it won't come off.

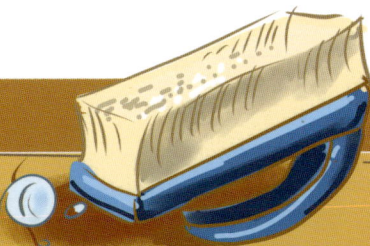

They have to pay a painter
to cover it all
and Eli feels bad
that he drew on the wall.

Says the painter,
"You should take care.
You can't just
scribble anywhere!"

Eli has learned
that paper is best.
Now when he colors
there is no mess.
He wants the walls
to stay clean and white
so his house
will look just right!